Famous Immigrants

Debra J. Housel, M.S.Ed.

Publishing Credits

Historical Consultant
Shannon C. McCutchen

Editors
Wendy Conklin, M.A.
Torrey Maloof

Editorial Director
Emily R. Smith, M.A.Ed.

Editor-in-Chief
Sharon Coan, M.S.Ed.

Creative Director
Lee Aucoin

Illustration Manager
Timothy J. Bradley

Publisher
Rachelle Cracchiolo, M.S.Ed.

Teacher Created Materials
5301 Oceanus Drive
Huntington Beach, CA 92649-1030
http://www.tcmpub.com

ISBN 978-0-7439-0663-0

Printed in Malaysia
Thumbprints.42806

Table of Contents

On the Move

In the 1800s and early 1900s, millions of **immigrants** moved to the United States. They were searching for a better life. Back home, they lived poor lives and were often hungry. They had little hope of having better lives if they stayed. Some people were not allowed to talk about what they believed. Others had to deal with wars waging around them.

On top of all that, Europe was too crowded. The people there heard of jobs and lots of available land across the ocean. People left behind everything. Some people sold all they owned to buy ship tickets.

Huge crowds entered the United States daily. They hoped to get jobs and own homes. They wanted to worship in their own ways. Many had their hopes fulfilled. These immigrants went on to change the United States into the nation it is today.

These men board a ship to travel from Italy to the United States in 1900.

An Exploding Population!

By 1860, four million immigrants had already entered the nation. And this was before the Great Migration years of 1900–1930!

Walt Whitman Says . . .

Walt Whitman was a famous poet. He described the United States with these words: "Here is not merely a nation, but a **teeming** nation of nations." In other words, the United States is made up of people from all over the world.

The Statue of Liberty welcomed immigrants to America.

I Don't Want to Go!

Most Africans did not choose to **emigrate**. Millions were kidnapped and taken overseas. Then they were sold into slavery.

Canadian Immigrants

Elijah McCoy is not the only well-known person who emigrated from Canada. Wayne Gretzky, who played for many years in the National Hockey League, is Canadian. There are also a number of entertainers who were born in Canada—Michael J. Fox, William Shatner, Alex Trebek, and Neil Young, to name a few.

Africans were captured and forced to go to the Americas as slaves.

Elijah McCoy was from Ontario, Canada. Ontario is north of Wisconsin and Michigan.

A Canadian Immigrant

Most boys love trains and Elijah McCoy was no different. Until the 1840s, his parents were slaves in Kentucky. They ran away to freedom on the **Underground Railroad**. They escaped to Ontario, Canada. That was where McCoy was born.

His parents knew that he was smart. So, they saved money to send him to Scotland at age 16. There, he was an **apprentice** (uh-PREN-tiss) to a mechanical engineer.

After that, McCoy moved to Michigan. He went to work for the railroad. Because he was an African American, he could only get a job as a **stoker**. The stokers kept steam locomotives going. They shoveled two tons (1.8 metric tons) of coal into the firebox each hour! It was the hottest and hardest job on a train. It was also the most dangerous.

Is This the Real McCoy?

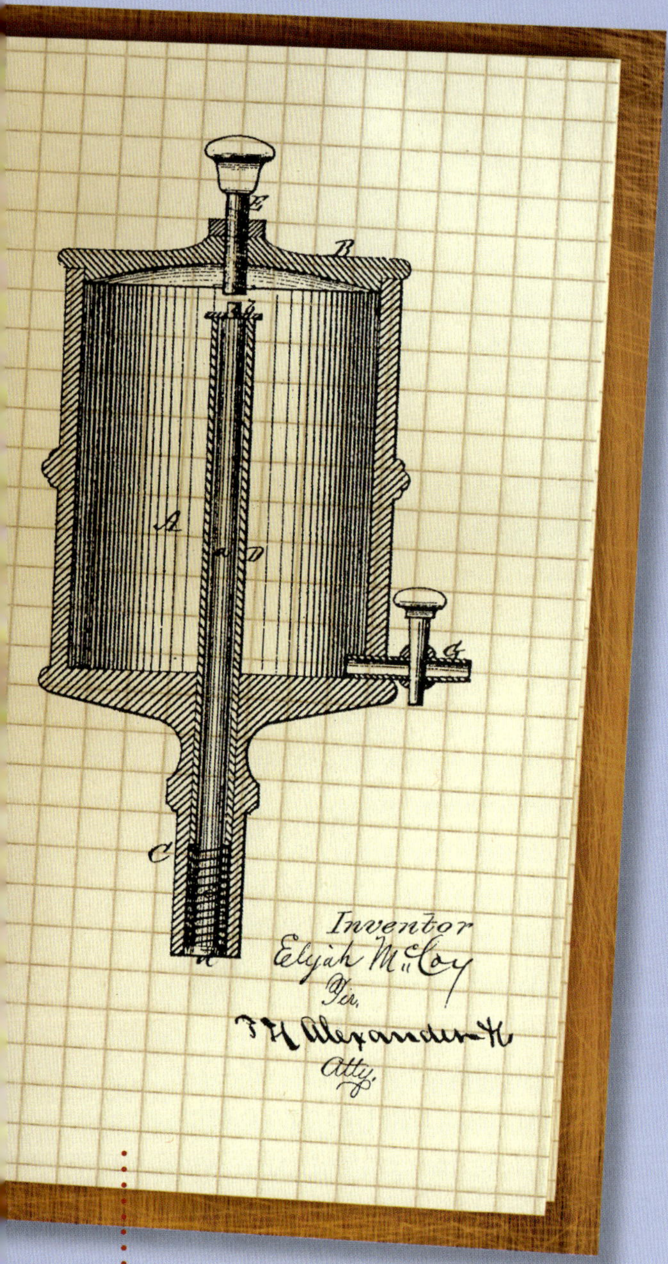

This is McCoy's drawing of his lubricating cup.

McCoy was in charge of oiling the engines, too. The engine had to stop often. It needed its moving parts oiled. Otherwise they would overheat. Sometimes one train would crash into another that had stopped for oiling.

McCoy knew there had to be a better way. So in 1872, he invented the first lubricating cup. It oiled the engine while it was still moving. This **revolutionized** (rev-uh-LOO-shuhn-ized) not only steam engines but other machines, too.

Over the years, he perfected his design. Other people tried to copy it. But no one else's was as good. When people bought a lubricator, they wanted to know, "Is this the real McCoy?" His name meant quality.

In 1916, he invented the graphite lubricator. It worked on the new, faster steamships and locomotives. McCoy was **inducted** into the National Inventors Hall of Fame in 2001.

More Inventions

McCoy married Mary Eleanora Delaney. For her, he invented the folding ironing board. It is still used today. He also made the first lawn sprinkler and created treads to improve tire **traction**.

Stay in School

McCoy loved children, although he had none of his own. Children were always welcome in his workshop. He gave them two pieces of advice: stay in school and work hard.

An old steam locomotive

Many Reasons

Pogroms were just one of the many reasons people left Europe. Others included war, hunger, poverty, and the chance to own land.

Name Change

Berlin was born Israel Baline. On one of his songs, his name was written down incorrectly as *I. Berlin*. He liked the sound of this new last name. He then chose Irving as his new first name.

A Russian Immigrant

In the 1800s, there were some groups of people who were killed because others thought they did not fit in. These massacres were called **pogroms** (POH-gruhms). Pogroms killed thousands of Jewish people in Europe.

Jewish people could not hold government jobs, own land, or travel. They even had to live in certain towns. Without warning, horrible rulers sent troops into those towns. The troops burned homes and beat people. When that happened, many families fled.

Irving Berlin's family was one of these families. They fled Russia for New York City in 1893. They lived in the dark, dirty basement of a **tenement** (TEN-uh-muhnt). The building was very overcrowded. Sickness spread easily. As a result, Berlin's father died in 1896.

His mother did **piecework**. She sewed pieces of clothing. When she finished a piece of clothing, she was paid for it. It was hard for her to earn enough money to feed the family. So in 1901, Berlin left home. He was just 13.

These Russian immigrants just arrived in the United States.

Sometimes, everyone in a family did piecework together.

A Vaudeville Singer

Berlin knew that it would be hard to live on his own. He had great musical talent but no training. So, he stood on a street corner and sang. A man asked Berlin to sing in his bar. That was Berlin's first job.

Soon, another man heard Berlin singing. He hired Berlin as a song plugger at **vaudeville** (VAWD-vuhl) shows. In those days, there was no radio or television. Music was always live performances. People went to vaudeville shows to see dancing and singing. As soon as a song ended on stage, Berlin's job was to jump on stage and sing

A vaudeville theater in New York City

Irving Berlin composed many well-known songs.

it again. Then, the people would buy the sheet music to play on their pianos at home.

Berlin thought that formal training might hinder his success. So, he never learned to read or write music. He played the piano by ear. When Berlin created a new song, he sang or played it for someone else. That person wrote down the musical notes.

Berlin's Family

Berlin married Ellin Mackay. She was a Christian. Since he was Jewish, her parents disapproved of the match. After a few years, they did accept him.

Honors for Berlin

In 1942, Berlin won an Academy Award® for his song, "White Christmas." It's still popular more than 60 years later. Later, President Dwight Eisenhower awarded him a congressional medal for "God Bless America."

Music Was Good for His Soul

Berlin was America's most **prolific** (pruh-LIF-ik) songwriter. That means he wrote more music than any other American. Berlin wrote the scores for 20 musicals and more than 1,500 songs. He published 900 of those, and about half of them were big hits! He lived to be 101 years old.

A Polish Rose

Rose Schneiderman (SHEE-duh-man) was born in Poland. In 1891, the Schneiderman family **immigrated** to New York City. Soon after their arrival, Mr. Schneiderman died. This left the family with very little money. Young Rose had to drop out of school. She had to get a job. Schneiderman started working in the garment district. She was shocked by the horrible working conditions. When she was 21, Schneiderman organized a trade union.

In 1928, Schneiderman became president of the Women's Trade Union League. During her lifetime, she fought hard to improve the working conditions of others, especially women. All her hard work did not go unnoticed. First Lady Eleanor Roosevelt was one of Schneiderman's biggest supporters and closest friends.

Broadway is a famous street in New York City where people can see plays and musicals.

America's Song and Dance Man

In 1911, Berlin wrote "Alexander's Ragtime Band." This song sparked a dancing craze. The ragtime dance was just two steps. Before that, people had to learn the many steps to a polka or a waltz. At every dance hall, his song played over and over again.

Berlin had a knack for knowing what people liked. In 1919, he went into business. He grew rich fast. Berlin opened Music Box Theater on Broadway in 1921. Its first show made $500,000! That was a lot of money at that time.

During World War II, Berlin wrote "God Bless America." All of the money it made went to the Boy Scouts and Girl Scouts. Then, he wrote the musical *This Is the Army*. He gave the $10 million it earned to help the United States troops.

This is an advertisement for an Irving Berlin production.

An Irish Immigrant

Edward Flanagan had a big family. One of his sisters lived in New York City. She told him that America was a great place. So, he emigrated from Ireland to the United States in 1904. He was 18 years old.

Even as a child, Flanagan knew that he wanted to be a Roman Catholic priest. His brother was already a priest. As soon as he arrived in America, Flanagan enrolled in a **seminary** (SEM-uh-nair-ee). But he soon fell ill. He was sent home. He tried to return to his studies three times. Each time he got **pneumonia** (noo-MOH-nyuh) and almost died.

Overcrowded ships led to sickness at sea.

People tried to talk him out of being a priest. They said he did not have strong enough health. But Flanagan was determined. At last, he went to Austria. The weather there agreed with him. He was **ordained** in 1912. He was finally a priest!

The Coffin Ships

The worst conditions on ships coming to America were the Irish "coffin ships." Many people were ill or starving when they boarded. They were told to bring their own food, but they had none to bring!

The Potato Famine

Ireland had a **famine** (FAM-uhn) from 1845–1850. Most of the Irish were poor. Their main food was potatoes. When the crops failed, one-fourth of the nation starved. This famine forced many Irish people to immigrate to America.

Tough Luck

When people fell on hard times, they had to rely on family or friends for help. If a boy did not have this, he had to get by as best as he could on his own. Sometimes that meant he had to break the law.

Father Flanagan's Beliefs

Father Flanagan had a slogan: "There is no such thing as a bad boy." He also said, "There can be no peace of mind unless there is a piece of bread."

Homeless boys got into trouble and often stole food to survive.

Father Flanagan Finds His Mission

Flanagan returned to America as a priest. People called him Father Flanagan. But he wanted to do more than just help people in his church. He wanted to help **drifters** who wandered from town to town. So, he fixed a rundown hotel into a place for them to stay.

During this time, Flanagan saw that there were many homeless boys. They roamed the streets and stole food. He thought of his own happy childhood. He believed that if these boys had homes and felt loved, they would grow to be good citizens.

Flanagan borrowed $90 to rent an old house. In 1917, he took in five boys. Within two weeks, 20 more boys had moved in. The house was crowded. Still, Flanagan begged the courts not to send the boys to jail. He told them that he would take care of the boys.

Father Flanagan wanted the boys to feel safe and loved.

These are the first five boys helped by Father Flanagan.

Boys' Town—Here We Come!

People admired what Flanagan was doing. Bakers offered him day-old rolls. Farmers gave him cows for milk. People gave clothing, furnishings, and food. Women volunteered to cook meals and clean. Somehow, he scraped together the monthly rent.

More boys poured through the doors. Peer pressure controlled their actions. They encouraged each other to behave. No one wanted to go back to the streets!

By 1921, Flanagan had helped more than a thousand boys from 17 states. In that same year, Flanagan bought a large farm. On it he built a place called Boys' Home. In 1926, the name was changed to Boys' Town.

Food and livestock grew in the fields. There was a hospital, a chapel, classrooms, and a barber shop. There was also a wood shop and machine shop. The boys learned trades or how to farm. This way, they learned to take care of themselves.

The people at Boys' Town helped thousands of boys.

The original front gate of Boys' Home

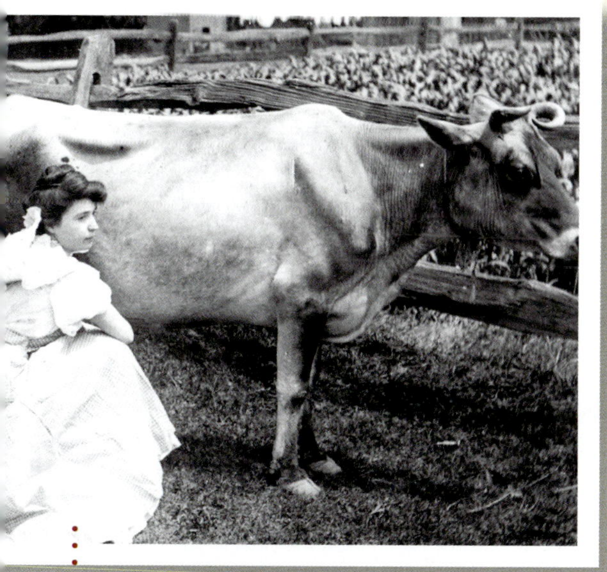

Farmers donated their milk cows to Boys' Town.

"Mother" Mary

Mary Harris was born in Ireland. Her family left their home in 1835 to escape British rule. As an adult, Harris became a teacher and married George Jones. Her husband told her about the horrible conditions in the factory where he worked. Sadly, Mary Jones's husband and four children all died of yellow fever.

To start over, Jones moved to Chicago and became a dressmaker. Then, she began to help men and women fight for better working conditions. People began calling her Mother Jones. She became well known for helping coal miners and children. She once organized a march from Pennsylvania to the home of President Franklin Roosevelt in New York. The children carried banners that said, "We want time to play! We want to go to school!" Mother Jones worked hard fighting for the rights of others.

Chinese immigrants tend to their farms in California.

Hard Workers

Many people did not like the Chinese. At one time, no one would hire them. So the resourceful Chinese opened restaurants and laundries.

Treatment of Asians

In 1920, no Asian immigrants could own land in the United States. They were not allowed to become U.S. citizens. They could not even marry white people. It took a long time to change these unfair laws.

A Chinese Immigrant

The gold rush in 1849 lured Chinese men to California. But to emigrate from China, they had to sneak aboard ships. Their rulers did not want them to go. If caught, the men faced death. America needed workers for railroads and mines. So, the risk was worth it to them.

Chinese immigrant children in California faced many difficulties.

In 1882, Congress passed the Chinese Exclusion Act. It stopped emigration from China to the United States. Only a small number of Chinese could come into the nation each year.

Ieoh Ming Pei (EE-oh MING PAY) was one of these. Pei was allowed to enter as a student in 1935. **Clergy**, **diplomats**, and teachers could also come. Pei's father said he could get the best education in America. Pei had always liked to watch tall buildings going up. So, he came to the United States to study **architecture** (ARE-kuh-tek-chuhr).

World-Famous Architect

Pei married Eileen Loo in 1942. He and his wife planned to go home to China. But the government in China grew unstable. The Peis decided to stay in the United States for good.

Pei became a U.S. citizen in 1954. A year later he started his own architecture firm. His designs were exciting. And he did things on time and on budget. He was always busy.

One of Pei's most popular designs is the Rock and Roll Hall of Fame and Museum. The other is an addition to the Louvre (LOO-vruh) in France. The Louvre is the most famous art museum in the world. Not everyone likes his modern pyramids at this historic museum.

In 1979, he won the Gold Medal of the American Institute of Architects. It is the highest award in his field.

Chinese Scientist

Chien-Shiung Wu (chee-en-SHE-uhng WOO) was born in China. After graduating from college, Wu emigrated to the United States in 1936. She wanted to study science. She received another degree from a university in California. She soon became known as an expert in her field. She was the first female instructor at Princeton University.

A few months later, Columbia University asked Wu to come work on a top-secret project. It was called the Manhattan Project. Its goal was to develop the first atomic bomb. Scientists were having trouble with a particular part of the project. Wu found a solution to the problem. This atomic bomb was later used during World War II.

The Rock and Roll Hall of Fame and Museum in Cleveland, Ohio, is very unique.

The pyramids at the Louvre in Paris, France, are controversial.

Wu is one of the most famous female scientists in history.

Other Amazing Immigrants

Levi Strauss came from Bavaria (buh-VAR-ee-uh) in 1843. He started making jeans for gold miners. They needed sturdy pants. The design of the pants has changed very little over the years.

In 1893, Knute Rockne came from Norway. In 1918, he became the head coach of the Notre Dame football team. From 1918–1930, his team set the greatest all-time winning percentage. He had 105 wins, 12 losses, 5 ties, and 6 national championships. That's an amazing record!

Louis B. Mayer was Jewish. He fled Russia in 1904. He made his first film in 1918. Five years later, he was one of the cofounders of MGM Studios. Later, he helped create the Academy of Motion Picture Arts and Sciences in 1927. Each year, this group gives out Academy Awards® to the top stars, films, and filmmakers.

First Female Secretary of State

Madeleine Albright was born in Czechoslovakia (chek-uh-slow-VAW-kee-uh). The Albright family immigrated to the United States in 1948. They were trying to escape Communist rule. Albright worked very hard in school. In 1959, she graduated from college. She went on to earn two more degrees. Albright then became a professor at Georgetown University.

In 1993, Albright was named the U.S. ambassador to the United Nations. President William Clinton named Albright the United States secretary of state in 1997. She was the first woman to serve in this important role.

The Notre Dame football team is very popular around the country.

A gold miner needed strong pants that would not tear easily.

The back lot of MGM Studios is where many movies are filmed.

Other Amazing Immigrants *(cont.)*

Jokichi Takamine (joe-KEE-chee tok-uh-MEEN-ee) was a scientist from Japan. He arrived in America in 1894. He set up a laboratory in New Jersey. His lab researched medicine for the human body. In 1901, he found the human hormone adrenaline (uh-DREN-uh-luhn). It is called epinephrine (eh-puh-NEH-fruhn). This is the fluid in EpiPens®. These are carried by people with severe allergic reactions to food or bugs.

Kahlil Gibran (kaw-LEEL juh-BRAWN) was a world-famous author. He wrote about peace and tolerance. He believed that love was the most important thing. His best-known work is *The Prophet*. He was born in Lebanon and immigrated to the United States in 1895.

Kahlil Gibran was a thoughtful boy.

Thousands of immigrants have done great things in the United States. Many of their names have been forgotten. But each immigrant added to what America is today. The food we eat, the way we speak, the music we love, and even the values we have—like freedom of speech—are based on ideas brought here from around the world.

Immigrants protest the policies in the United States.

Questions for the Future

Immigration is still a hot topic. Many of the same questions that have been discussed for a century continue to be debated. Who should be allowed to come into America? Who should be excluded? How do we teach these new Americans?

From All Over

Immigrants continue to come to America. Each year about one million people enter the country. Today, most immigrants come from Mexico, the Philippines, Russia, and China.

An immigrant carries all he owns in his trunk.

Glossary

apprentice—someone who learns a trade by working with a skilled person

architecture—the art of designing buildings

clergy—people trained to lead religious services, such as priests, rabbis, and ministers

diplomats—people representing their nations' governments in foreign countries

drifters—people who wander from place to place without fixed homes or jobs

emigrate—to leave a place of residence to live somewhere new

famine—extreme lack of food

immigrants—people who come to new nations to live

immigrated—moved to a new place of residence

inducted—entered into, made part of

ordained—brought into a religious ministry or the priesthood

piecework—work where wages are earned based on the number of pieces sewed

pneumonia—a serious illness that causes the lungs to fill with a thick fluid, which makes it hard to breathe

pogroms—organized killings of groups of people for political or religious reasons; usually planned by government leaders

prolific—creating many works

revolutionized—completely changed

seminary—a college that teaches students to become priests or ministers

stoker—the fireman on a steam locomotive whose job it was to keep the engine running

teeming—full of something

tenement—a run-down apartment building in a poor section of a city

traction—gripping power that keeps a moving thing from sliding on a slippery surface

Underground Railroad—secret system that helped slaves escape north

vaudeville—a type of entertainment that features live musical and comedy acts

Index

Image Credits

cover Culver Pictures, Inc./SuperStock; p.1 Culver Pictures, Inc./SuperStock; pp.4–5 The Granger Collection, New York; p.5 Mike Liu/Shutterstock, Inc.; p.6 (top) The Bridgeman Art Library/Getty Images; p.6 (bottom) The Granger Collection, New York; p.7 Courtesy of Tracy Sugarman; p.8 U.S. Patent Office; p.9 (left) Gregor GP Buir/Shutterstock, Inc.; p.9 (right) Thomas Mounsey/Shutterstock, Inc.; p.10 Mary Evans Picture Library/Alamy; p.11 The Library of Congress; p.12 The Granger Collection, New York; p.13 Culver Pictures, Inc./SuperStock; p.14 (left) The Library of Congress; p.14 (right) byphoto/Shutterstock, Inc.; pp.14–15 Pictorial Press Ltd/Alamy; pp.16–17 The Granger Collection, New York; p.17 Peter Jochems/Shutterstock, Inc.; p.18 The Library of Congress; p.19 (top) Girls and Boys Town Hall of History Collection; p.19 (bottom) Girls and Boys Town Hall of History Collection; p.20 Girls and Boys Town Hall of History Collection; p.21 (top) Girls and Boys Town Hall of History Collection; p.21 (bottom) The Library of Congress; p.22 The Granger Collection, New York; p.23 The Granger Collection, New York; p.24 Beau Wade/flickr.com; p.25 (left) Robert Daveant/Shutterstock, Inc.; p.25 (right) Bettmann/Corbis; p.27 (top left) Jeremy R. Smith/Shutterstock, Inc.; p.27 (top right) Corbis; p.27 (bottom) Hulton Archive/Getty Images; p.28 The Library of Congress; p.29 (left) Mark Scott Spatney/Shutterstock, Inc.; p.29 (right) Corbis